My Pew: Things I have seen from it

Also available from Canterbury Press

The Dave Walker Guide to the Church

'Dave helps us laugh at ourselves . . . and he may even be a catalyst for change, although of course if we became too normal we'd put him out of business . . . his cartoons are works of genius.' *Christian Marketplace*

The Dave Walker Guide to the Church Calendar

An annual favourite to help you emerge smiling from the rigours of the church year.

www.canterburypress.co.uk

MY PEW

*Things I have
seen from it*

Dave Walker

CANTERBURY
PRESS
Norwich

First published in 2008 by the Canterbury Press Norwich
(a publishing imprint of Hymns Ancient & Modern Limited,
a registered charity)
13–17 Long Lane, London EC1A 9PN

www.scm-canterburypress.co.uk

British Library Cataloguing in Publication data

A catalogue record for this book is available
from the British Library

ISBN 978-1-85311-899-9

Printed in the UK by
CPI William Clowes, Beccles, NR34 7TL

INTRODUCTION

TO THIS, MY SECOND BOOK OF DIAGRAMS

HUMOROUS ANECDOTE INCLUDED FOR THE SAKE OF IT →

← SUMMARY OF THE MAIN FINDINGS

ACCOUNT OF THE MANY LONG NIGHTS OF TOIL →

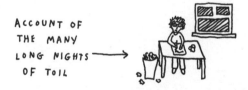

← PEOPLE I WOULD LIKE TO THANK FOR ONE REASON OR ANOTHER

DEEPLY PROFOUND OBSERVATION →

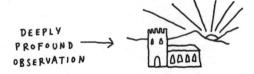

DAVE WALKER

THE SERVICE

CAUSES OF JOY AND SORROW

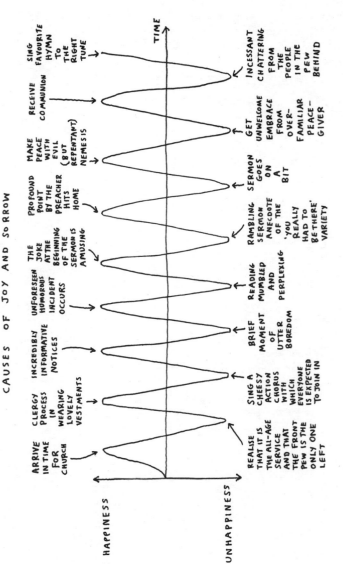

HAPPINESS

UNHAPPINESS

TIME

ARRIVE IN TIME FOR CHURCH

CLERGY PROCESS IN WEARING LOVELY VESTMENTS

INCREDIBLY INFORMATIVE NOTICES

UNFORESEEN HUMOROUS INCIDENT OCCURS

THE JOKE AT THE BEGINNING OF THE SERMON IS AMUSING

PROFOUND POINT BY THE PREACHER HITS HOME

MAKE PEACE WITH EVIL (BUT REPENTANT) NEMESIS

RECEIVE COMMUNION

SING FAVOURITE HYMN TO THE RIGHT TUNE

REALISE THAT IT IS THE ALL-AGE SERVICE AND THAT THE FRONT PEW IS THE ONLY ONE LEFT

SING A CHEESY ACTION CHORUS WITH WHICH EVERYONE IS EXPECTED TO JOIN IN

BRIEF MOMENT OF UTTER BOREDOM

READING MUMBLED AND PERPLEXING

RAMBLING SERMON ANECDOTE OF THE 'YOU REALLY HAD TO BE THERE' VARIETY

SERMON GOES ON A BIT

GET UNWELCOME EMBRACE FROM OVER-FAMILIAR PEACE-GIVER

INCESSANT CHATTERING FROM THE PEOPLE IN THE PEW BEHIND

WORSHIP

THIS SHOULD INVOLVE ALL OF THE SENSES

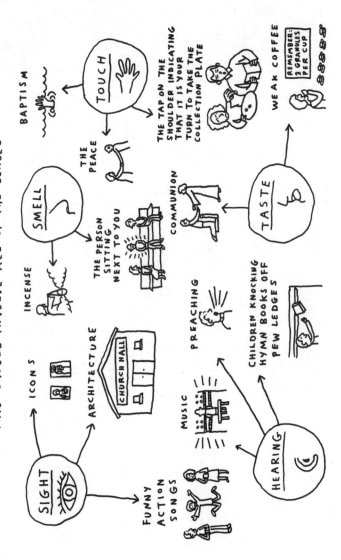

THE WELCOMERS

IT IS THE
JOB OF THE
WELCOMERS
TO BE
WELCOMING
AND WEAR
A BADGE

THEY ARE
GIVEN
IN-DEPTH
TRAINING
TO EQUIP
THEM FOR
THIS ROLE

IN THE
EVENT
OF ANY
NEWCOMERS
ATTENDING
A SERVICE
A WELCOMER
WILL BE
SUMMONED
TO DEAL
WITH THE
SITUATION

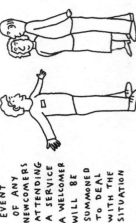

THERE IS
A ROTA
SO THAT
THE SAME
PEOPLE
DO NOT
HAVE TO BE
WELCOMING
EVERY WEEK

THE WELCOME PACK

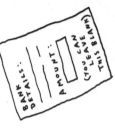

THE STANDING
ORDER FORM...

AND THE COMBINATION
CODE FOR THE TOILETS

THIS CONTAINS THE
RULES AND REGULATIONS...

THE SMALL
PRINT...

NEWCOMERS ARE GIVEN
A WELCOME PACK

THE 'VOLUNTEERING'
FORM...

FINDING A SEAT

THERE IS USUALLY ENOUGH ROOM IF EVERYBODY MOVES ALONG THE PEW A LITTLE BIT

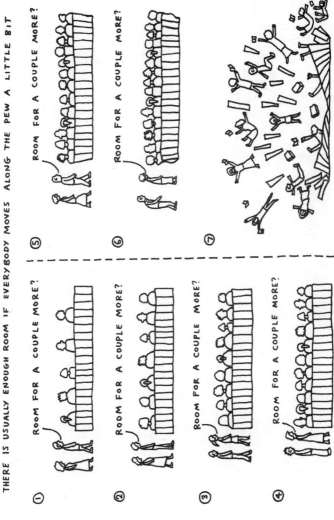

① ROOM FOR A COUPLE MORE?

② ROOM FOR A COUPLE MORE?

③ ROOM FOR A COUPLE MORE?

④ ROOM FOR A COUPLE MORE?

⑤ ROOM FOR A COUPLE MORE?

⑥ ROOM FOR A COUPLE MORE?

⑦

PROCESSIONS

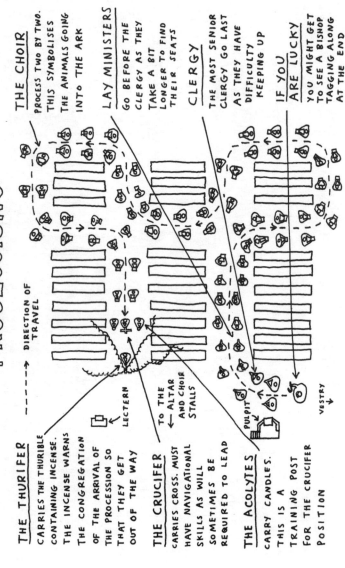

------> DIRECTION OF TRAVEL

LECTERN

TO THE ALTAR AND CHOIR STALLS

PULPIT

VESTRY

THE THURIFER

CARRIES THE THURIBLE CONTAINING INCENSE. THE INCENSE WARNS THE CONGREGATION OF THE ARRIVAL OF THE PROCESSION SO THAT THEY GET OUT OF THE WAY

THE CRUCIFER

CARRIES CROSS. MUST HAVE NAVIGATIONAL SKILLS AS WILL SOMETIMES BE REQUIRED TO LEAD

THE ACOLYTES

CARRY CANDLES. THIS IS A TRAINING POST FOR THE CRUCIFER POSITION

THE CHOIR

PROCESS TWO BY TWO. THIS SYMBOLISES THE ANIMALS GOING INTO THE ARK

LAY MINISTERS

GO BEFORE THE CLERGY AS THEY TAKE A BIT LONGER TO FIND THEIR SEATS

CLERGY

THE MOST SENIOR CLERGY GO LAST AS THEY HAVE DIFFICULTY KEEPING UP

IF YOU ARE LUCKY

YOU MIGHT GET TO SEE A BISHOP TAGGING ALONG AT THE END

ECCLESIASTICAL WALKING

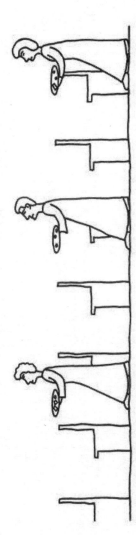

THOSE UNDERTAKING LITURGICAL DUTIES MUST WALK IN A SLOW AND DIGNIFIED MANNER

THIS ECCLESIASTICAL WALK MUST BE PRACTISED AT EVERY OPPORTUNITY

HYMNS

IT IS QUITE EASY TO JOIN IN

① FIRST OF ALL FIND
THE RIGHT BOOK

② THEN FIND THE
RIGHT NUMBER

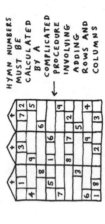

HYMN NUMBERS
MUST BE
CALCULATED
BY A
COMPLICATED
PROCEDURE
INVOLVING
ADDING
ROWS AND
COLUMNS

③ BE SURE YOU ARE SINGING
THE RIGHT TUNE

④ MAKE SURE YOU FOLLOW
THE VERSE NUMBERS CAREFULLY

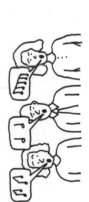

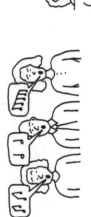

(IT CAN BE EMBARRASSING TO KEEP
SINGING WHEN EVERYONE ELSE HAS STOPPED)

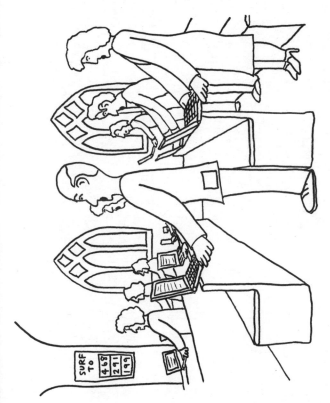

THESE DAYS WE DO NOT NEED HYMN BOOKS
AS ALL OF THE WORDS TO THE SONGS
CAN BE FOUND ON THE INTERNET

KEEPING ORDER

IT IS IMPORTANT TO MAINTAIN DISCIPLINE DURING SERVICES.
THESE ARE SOME OF THE PENALTIES FOR COMMON MISDEMEANOURS

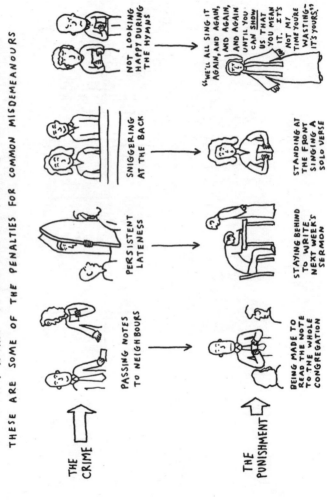

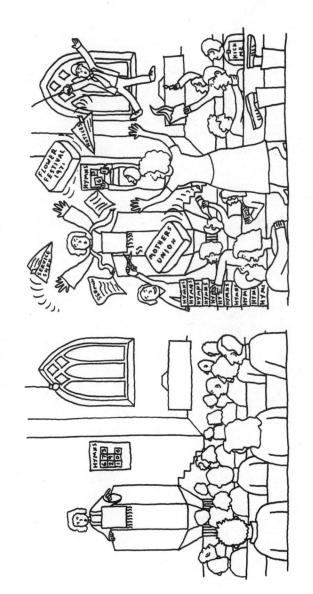

THE SERMON

PEOPLE MAY HAVE THEIR EYES CLOSED FOR A NUMBER OF REASONS

UP EARLY PRAYING (FOR TAX COLLECTORS AND SINNERS)

UP LATE PARTYING (WITH TAX COLLECTORS AND SINNERS)

ALREADY HEARD SERMON THE LAST TIME IT WAS USED

ALREADY READ SERMON ON THE PREACHER'S BLOG

VISUALISING BIBLE PASSAGE IN QUIETNESS OF OWN HEART

HAPPENED TO BE BLINKING AT THE MOMENT CARTOON WAS DRAWN

BORED SENSELESS

THE SERMON

THERE ARE SOME PEOPLE WHO ARE NOT IN THE DIRECT
LINE OF FIRE AS FAR AS THE SERMON IS CONCERNED

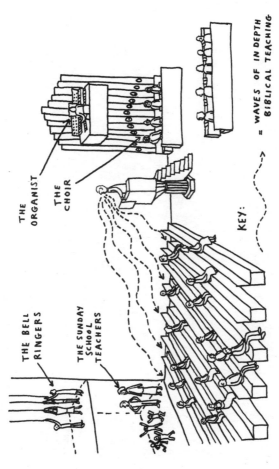

THE BELL
RINGERS

THE SUNDAY
SCHOOL
TEACHERS

THE
ORGANIST

THE
CHOIR

KEY:

---> = WAVES OF IN DEPTH
        BIBLICAL TEACHING

THESE PEOPLE SHOULD BE VISITED REGULARLY FOR
A CHAT ABOUT RECENT SERMON TOPICS

THE PEACE

IT IS TRADITIONAL FOR EVERYONE IN THE CHURCH TO SHAKE
THE HAND OF EVERY OTHER PERSON IN THE CHURCH

IN A CONGREGATION
OF 20 THERE
WILL BE <u>190</u>
PEACEFUL
INTERACTIONS

IN A CONGREGATION
OF 50 THERE
WILL BE <u>1225</u>
PEACEFUL
INTERACTIONS

IN A CONGREGATION
OF 100 THERE
WILL BE <u>4950</u>
PEACEFUL
INTERACTIONS

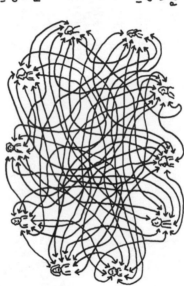

THIS DIAGRAM
SHOWS THE <u>45</u>
PEACEFUL
INTERACTIONS
THAT TAKE
PLACE WHEN
EVERYONE IN
A CONGREGATION
OF TEN SHAKES
HANDS WITH
EVERYONE ELSE

<u>FORMULA THAT CAN BE USED TO IMPRESS PEOPLE AT PARTIES:</u>

THE TOTAL NUMBER OF PEACEFUL INTERACTIONS IS $N \times \left(\dfrac{N-1}{2}\right)$

WHERE 'N' IS THE NUMBER OF CONGREGANTS

THE COLLECTION

YOU CAN
PUT IN
SOME
COINS

OR
SOME
NOTES

OR FILL IN
A DIRECT
DEBIT FORM

BUT SECRETLY
THE CHURCH
AUTHORITIES
WOULD PREFER
A DONATION OF
FRESH PRODUCE

COMMUNION

SIMPLIFIED DIAGRAM EXPLAINING THE ROUTES
YOU MUST TAKE

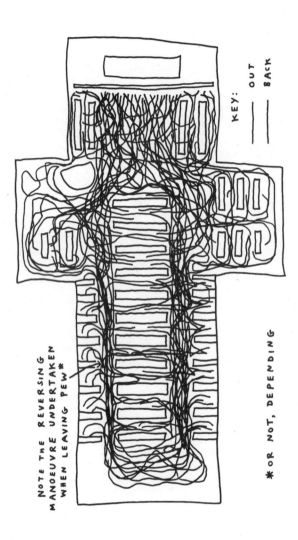

NOTE THE REVERSING
MANOEUVRE UNDERTAKEN
WHEN LEAVING PEW*

KEY:
——— OUT
——— BACK

*OR NOT, DEPENDING

COMMUNION WINE

THE NUMBER OF PEOPLE IN THE CONGREGATION	THE AMOUNT OF WINE THAT THE PRIEST HAS TO FINISH

PLEASE COME TO CHURCH SO THAT THE PRIEST CAN DRIVE HOME SAFELY

AFTER-SERVICE COFFEE

THIS IS THE TIME WHEN NEWCOMERS CAN GET TO KNOW THE CONGREGATION

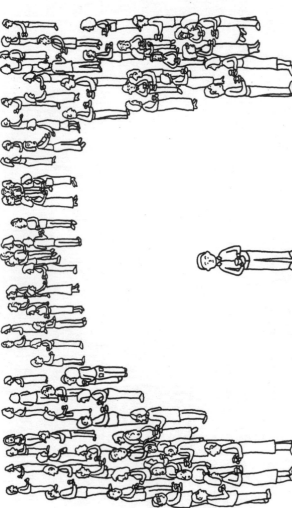

FIXTURES AND FITTINGS

THAT YOU MAY HAVE OBSERVED DURING THE SERVICES

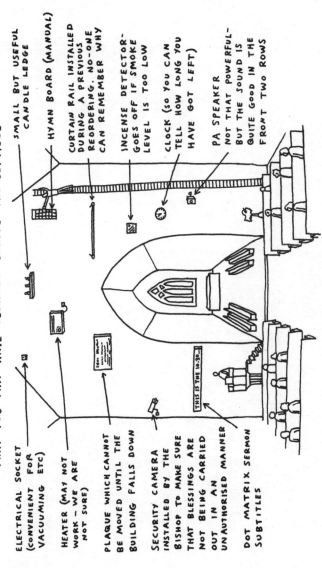

SMALL BUT USEFUL CANDLE LEDGE

HYMN BOARD (MANUAL)

CURTAIN RAIL INSTALLED DURING A PREVIOUS REORDERING. NO-ONE CAN REMEMBER WHY

INCENSE DETECTOR - GOES OFF IF SMOKE LEVEL IS TOO LOW

CLOCK (SO YOU CAN TELL HOW LONG YOU HAVE GOT LEFT)

PA SPEAKER NOT THAT POWERFUL - BUT THE SOUND IS QUITE GOOD IN THE FRONT TWO ROWS

ELECTRICAL SOCKET (CONVENIENT FOR VACUUMING ETC)

HEATER (MAY NOT WORK - WE ARE NOT SURE)

PLAQUE WHICH CANNOT BE MOVED UNTIL THE BUILDING FALLS DOWN

SECURITY CAMERA INSTALLED BY THE BISHOP TO MAKE SURE THAT BLESSINGS ARE NOT BEING CARRIED OUT IN AN UNAUTHORISED MANNER

DOT MATRIX SERMON SUBTITLES

PEWS

THE FIVE WORST PLACES TO SIT, IN REVERSE ORDER:

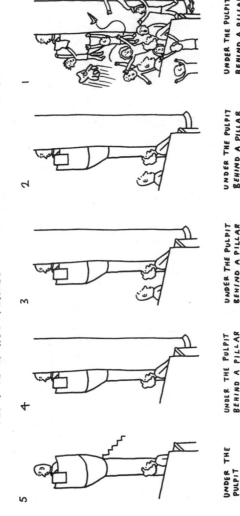

5
UNDER THE
PULPIT

4
UNDER THE PULPIT
BEHIND A PILLAR

3
UNDER THE PULPIT
BEHIND A PILLAR
NEXT TO THE
OUT-OF-TUNE
SINGER

2
UNDER THE PULPIT
BEHIND A PILLAR
NEXT TO THE
OUT-OF-TUNE
SINGER ON THE
NARROW PEW

1
UNDER THE PULPIT
BEHIND A PILLAR
NEXT TO THE
OUT-OF-TUNE
SINGER ON THE
NARROW PEW
NEAR THE
CHILDREN'S
CORNER

CHURCH SEATING

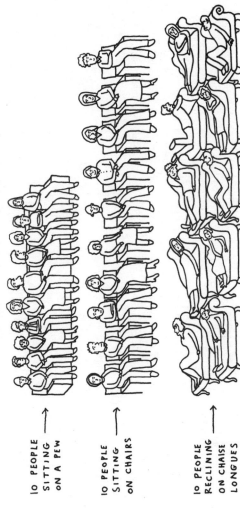

10 PEOPLE
SITTING
ON A PEW →

10 PEOPLE
SITTING
ON CHAIRS →

10 PEOPLE
RECLINING
ON CHAISE
LONGUES →

LESSONS LEARNT:

1. IT IS EASIER TO MAKE A CHURCH LOOK FULL IF THE PEWS ARE REPLACED BY CHAIRS

2. IT IS EVEN EASIER TO MAKE A CHURCH LOOK FULL IF THE PEWS ARE REPLACED BY CHAISE LONGUES

FURNITURE

IN THE OLD DAYS THE
ITEMS OF FURNITURE
WERE FIXED IN PLACE

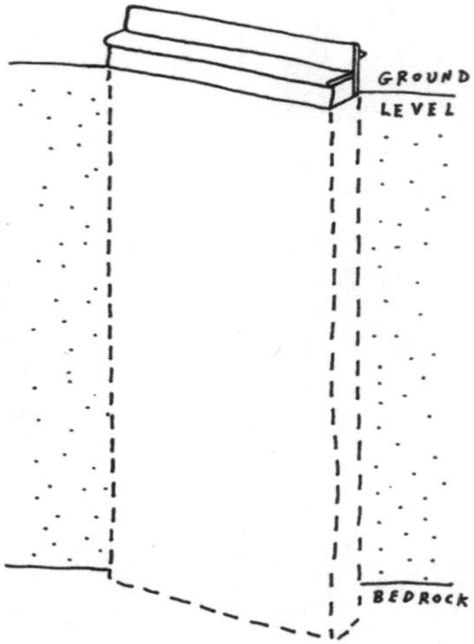

BUT NOW IN OUR MODERN AGE
THERE IS OFTEN A NEED
TO MOVE THINGS AROUND

MOBILE FONT

PULPIT ON WHEELS →

CHURCHWARDEN HAULING
A TRAIN OF PEWS

DIAGRAM SHOWING A PEW
AND ITS FOUNDATIONS

GROUND LEVEL

BEDROCK

THE CHOIR CAN
BE WHEELED IN
WHEN REQUIRED

THE YOUTH GROUP CAN
BE WHEELED OUT
WHEN NOT REQUIRED

DONATED ITEMS

OVER THE GENERATIONS A MULTITUDE OF
ITEMS HAVE BEEN GENEROUSLY DONATED

THESE ITEMS MUST BE USED REGULARLY
AND CANNOT EVER BE DISPOSED OF

LECTERNS

COLLECTION
PLATES

CANDLE STICKS

HYMN BOARDS

ALTAR CLOTHS

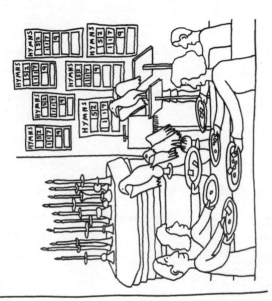

CURTAINS

THESE ARE USED AS FOLLOWS

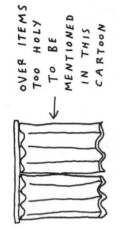

OVER THE
VESTRY DOOR
TO PRESERVE
THE MODESTY
OF THE
CLERGY

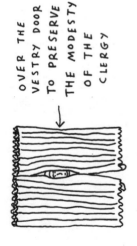

OVER THE
HYMN BOARD
TO ADD A
CERTAIN AMOUNT
OF SUSPENSE

OVER ITEMS
TOO HOLY
TO BE
MENTIONED
IN THIS
CARTOON

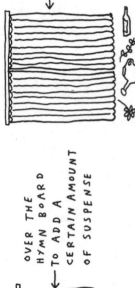

OVER THE
AREA WHERE
THE FLOWER
LADIES KEEP
THEIR BITS
AND BOBS

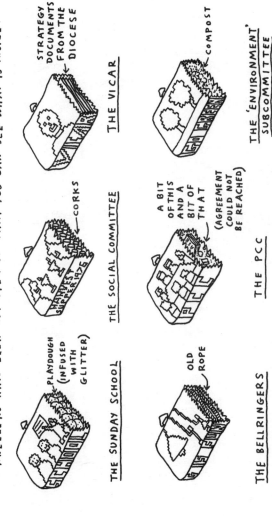

KNEELERS

Q. WHAT IS INSIDE THEM?

A. THE FILLING DEPENDS UPON WHO HAS MADE THE KNEELER. THESE KNEELERS HAVE BEEN CUT OPEN SO THAT YOU CAN SEE WHAT IS INSIDE:

STRATEGY DOCUMENTS FROM THE DIOCESE

THE VICAR

COMPOST

THE 'ENVIRONMENT' SUBCOMMITTEE

CORKS

THE SOCIAL COMMITTEE

A BIT OF THIS AND A BIT OF THAT

(AGREEMENT COULD NOT BE REACHED)

THE PCC

PLAYDOUGH (INFUSED WITH GLITTER)

THE SUNDAY SCHOOL

OLD ROPE

THE BELLRINGERS

IF YOU CONTINUE TO ABUSE THE KNEELERS WE WILL TAKE THEM AWAY

CHURCH SIGNS

HOW THE CHURCH CAN LEARN FROM THE RETAIL SECTOR

NEW TECHNOLOGY

HOW THE MODERN-DAY CHURCH IS USING IT

THE FAX MACHINE

NOTICE SHEETS
CAN BE
TRANSMITTED
VIA THE
TELEPHONE
LINE

THE PORTABLE AUDIOCASSETTE RECORDER

SERMONS
CAN BE
LISTENED-TO
AT ANY TIME
AND IN ANY
PLACE

THE HANDHELD LABELLING / EMBOSSING DEVICE

CHURCH
VALUABLES
CAN BE
LABELLED,
THUS
PREVENTING
THEM FROM
BEING
STOLEN

THIS FONT BELONGS TO

THE OVERHEAD PROJECTOR

THE WORDS
TO THE
HYMNS CAN
GO OVER
THE HEADS
OF THE
CONGREGATION

PROJECTION

THE 1950s:

THE SLIDE PROJECTOR

USED MAINLY BY MISSIONARIES GIVING INTERESTING TALKS

THE 1970s:

THE OVERHEAD PROJECTOR

USED TO PROJECT THE WORDS TO THE SONGS. REQUIRED ONE MEMBER OF THE CONGREGATION TO REMAIN ALERT DURING THE SERVICE TO CHANGE THE TRANSPARENCIES

THE 2000s:

THE DATA PROJECTOR

ATTACHED TO A LAPTOP COMPUTER, THEREBY DOUBLING THE NUMBER OF WAYS IT COULD GO WRONG

MY PREDICTION FOR THE FUTURE:

IT WILL BE FEASIBLE TO PRINT THE WORDS TO THE HYMNS, POSSIBLY IN BOOK FORM. PERHAPS EACH WORSHIPPER WILL BE ABLE TO HAVE THEIR OWN COPY

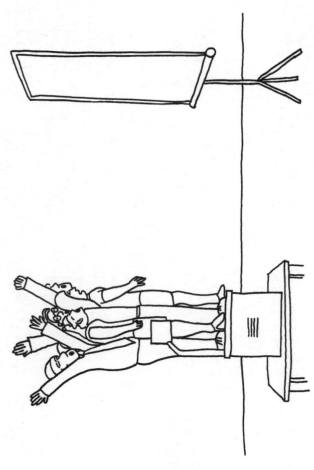

"WE WILL NOW STAND AND SING THE NEXT SONG ON THE OVERHEAD PROJECTOR"

CHURCH ARCHITECTURE

IT HAS BEEN NOTED THAT AFTER A WHILE CONGREGATION
MEMBERS BEGIN TO RESEMBLE THEIR CHURCH ARCHITECTURE

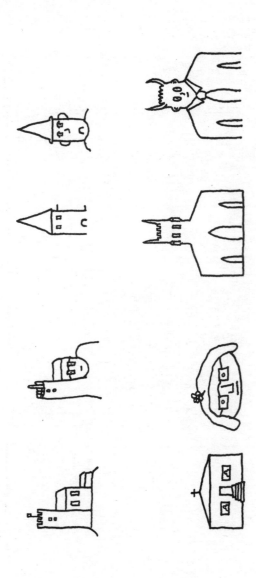

THE CHURCH TOWER

WAYS TO USE IT TO RAISE FUNDS

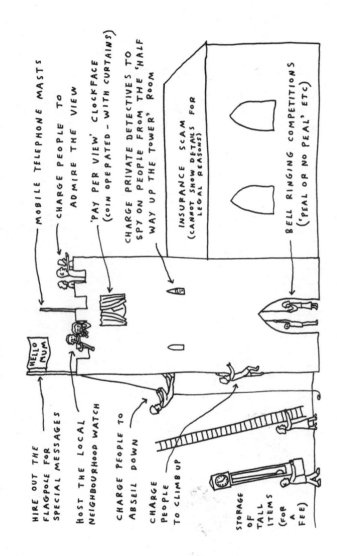

MOBILE TELEPHONE MASTS

CHARGE PEOPLE TO ADMIRE THE VIEW

'PAY PER VIEW' CLOCKFACE (COIN OPERATED – WITH CURTAINS)

CHARGE PRIVATE DETECTIVES TO SPY ON PEOPLE FROM THE 'HALF WAY UP THE TOWER' ROOM

INSURANCE SCAM (CANNOT SHOW DETAILS FOR LEGAL REASONS)

BELL RINGING COMPETITIONS ('PEAL OR NO PEAL' ETC)

HIRE OUT THE FLAGPOLE FOR SPECIAL MESSAGES

HELLO MUM

HOST THE LOCAL NEIGHBOURHOOD WATCH

CHARGE PEOPLE TO ABSEIL DOWN

CHARGE PEOPLE TO CLIMB UP

STORAGE OF TALL ITEMS (FOR A FEE)

FACULTIES

YOU WILL NEED TO ASK THE ARCHDEACON FOR ONE OF THESE IF
YOU HAVE PLANS TO DO ANY OF THE FOLLOWING:

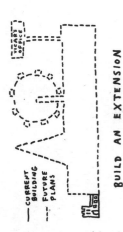

REPLACE THE PEWS WITH CHAIRS

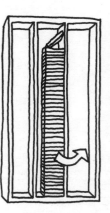

— CURRENT BUILDING
-- FUTURE PLANS

BUILD AN EXTENSION

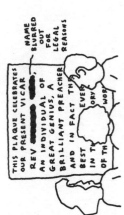

THIS PLAQUE CELEBRATES
OUR PRESENT VICAR
REV ███████, AN INDIVIDUAL OF
GREAT GENIUS, A
BRILLIANT PREACHER
AND IN FACT THE
BEST EVER
IN T...ORY
OF TH...WOR...

NAME
BLURRED
OUT
FOR
LEGAL
REASONS

PUT UP A PLAQUE

MOVE THE HYMN BOOKS THAT LIVE ON THE
SECOND SHELF ONTO THE FIRST SHELF

THE ANNUAL INSPECTION

THE CHURCHWARDENS MUST HAVE A LOOK AROUND THE CHURCH ONCE EVERY YEAR OR SO. THESE ARE THE SORTS OF THINGS THEY SHOULD BE LOOKING FOR:

SIGNS OF DANGER
(EG WIRING THAT DOES NOT LOOK QUITE RIGHT)

SIGNS OF LIFE

IT'LL HAVE TO COME DOWN — WE CAN'T RISK HAVING LEAVES IN THE GUTTERING

SIGNS OF MOVEMENT
(IN OLD BUILDINGS)

NO... NOTHING

SIGNS OF DEATH—
WATCH BEETLE

CHURCHWARDENS HAVE TO WATCH CLOSELY TO SPOT SIGNS OF CONTINUAL BORING

THE CHURCH PLAN

ALL CHURCHGOERS MUST MEMORISE THESE LOCATIONS SO THAT THEY CAN OBEY THE SIDESPERSON'S INSTRUCTIONS WITH A MINIMUM OF FUSS

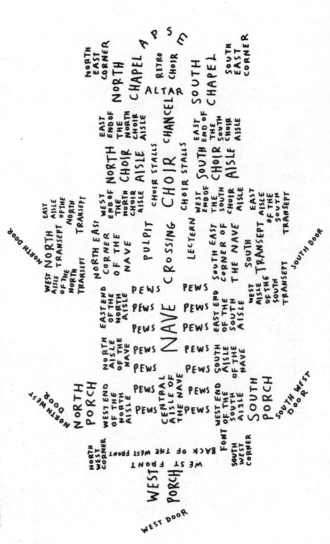

CHURCH SECURITY

SOME IDEAS TO MAKE IT BETTER

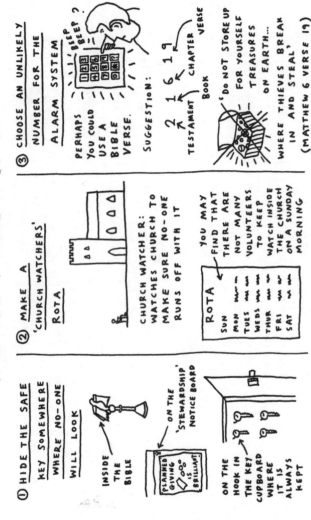

① HIDE THE SAFE KEY SOMEWHERE WHERE NO-ONE WILL LOOK

INSIDE THE BIBLE

ON THE 'STEWARDSHIP' NOTICE BOARD

PLANNED GIVING IS BRILLIANT

ON THE HOOK IN THE KEY CUPBOARD WHERE IT IS ALWAYS KEPT

② MAKE A 'CHURCH WATCHERS' ROTA

CHURCH WATCHER: WATCHES CHURCH TO MAKE SURE NO-ONE RUNS OFF WITH IT

ROTA
SUN
MON
TUES
WEDS
THUR
FRI
SAT

YOU MAY FIND THAT THERE ARE NOT MANY VOLUNTEERS TO KEEP WATCH INSIDE THE CHURCH ON A SUNDAY MORNING

③ CHOOSE AN UNLIKELY NUMBER FOR THE ALARM SYSTEM

BEEP BEEP ?

PERHAPS YOU COULD USE A BIBLE VERSE.

SUGGESTION:

2 1 6 19

TESTAMENT BOOK CHAPTER VERSE

'DO NOT STORE UP FOR YOURSELF TREASURES ON EARTH... WHERE THIEVES BREAK IN AND STEAL'

(MATTHEW 6 VERSE 19)

THE CHURCH BOILER

THERE ARE DIFFERENT SORTS

PAPER BURNING

DUBIOUS LIBERAL/
EVANGELICAL*
PAPERBACKS
ARE
SHOVELLED
IN

* TAKE YOUR PICK: BOTH SORTS WORK

PEDAL POWERED

NOTORIOUSLY INEFFICIENT, BUT THAT
DOES NOT MATTER AS CONGREGATION
KEEP WARM VIA THEIR OWN EXERTIONS

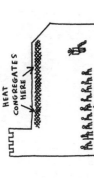

← ELABORATE PULLEY SYSTEM

COIN OPERATED

A DEPUTY UNDER-CHURCHWARDEN
SITS IN THE CRYPT
INSERTING A
10 PENCE PIECE
EVERY FEW
MINUTES

THE END RESULT

HEAT
CONGREGATES
HERE

CONGREGATION CONGREGATES HERE

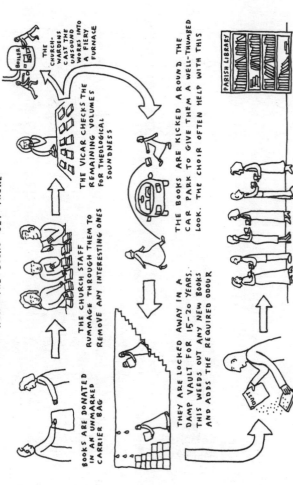

THE PARISH LIBRARY

HOW THE BOOKS GET THERE

BOOKS ARE DONATED IN AN UNMARKED CARRIER BAG

THE CHURCH STAFF RUMMAGE THROUGH THEM TO REMOVE ANY INTERESTING ONES

THE VICAR CHECKS THE REMAINING VOLUMES FOR THEOLOGICAL SOUNDNESS

THE CHURCH-WARDENS CAST THE UNSOUND WORKS INTO A FIERY FURNACE

BOILER

THE BOOKS ARE KICKED AROUND THE CAR PARK TO GIVE THEM A WELL-THUMBED LOOK. THE CHOIR OFTEN HELP WITH THIS

THEY ARE LOCKED AWAY IN A DAMP VAULT FOR 15-20 YEARS. THIS WEEDS OUT ANY NEW BOOKS AND ADDS THE REQUIRED ODOUR

SOME DUST IS ADDED

DUST

THE BOOKS CAN THEN BE ADDED TO THE SHELVES, GIVING THE CONGREGATION THE OPPORTUNITY TO IGNORE THEM

PARISH LIBRARY

THE CHURCH HALL

THE PEOPLE WHO USE IT AND THE DAMAGE THEY CAUSE

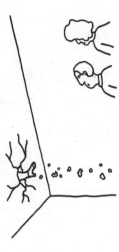

FLAMENCO DANCING GROUP: PUT HEELS
THROUGH THE FLOOR

MOTHERS AND TODDLERS: LEAVE STICKY
FINGER MARKS ON THE WALLS

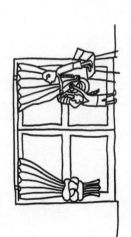

ARCHAEOLOGICAL SOCIETY: CARRY OUT
EXCAVATION WORK

SCOUTS: TIE KNOTS IN THINGS

THE VICARAGE WAITING ROOM

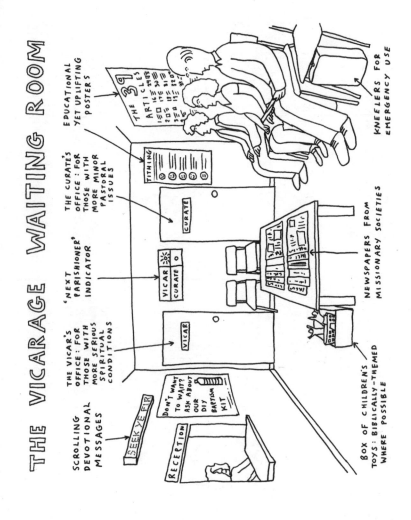

SCROLLING DEVOTIONAL MESSAGES

THE VICAR'S OFFICE: FOR THOSE WITH MORE SERIOUS SPIRITUAL CONDITIONS

'NEXT PARISHIONER' INDICATOR

THE CURATE'S OFFICE: FOR THOSE WITH MORE MINOR PASTORAL ISSUES

EDUCATIONAL YET UPLIFTING POSTERS

KNEELERS FOR EMERGENCY USE

NEWSPAPERS FROM MISSIONARY SOCIETIES

BOX OF CHILDREN'S TOYS: BIBLICALLY-THEMED WHERE POSSIBLE

DON'T WANT TO WAIT? ASK ABOUT OUR DIY BAPTISM KIT

SEEK YE FIR

RECEPTION

VICAR

CURATE

VICAR CURATE

TITHING

THE 39 ARTICLES

41

THE CLERICAL PENKNIFE

CLOSED

OPEN

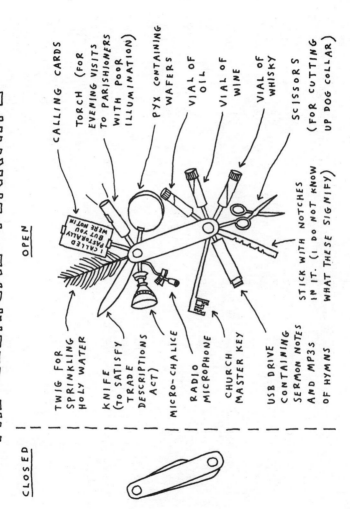

CALLING CARDS

TORCH (FOR EVENING VISITS TO PARISHIONERS WITH POOR ILLUMINATION)

PYX CONTAINING WAFERS

VIAL OF OIL

VIAL OF WINE

VIAL OF WHISKY

SCISSORS (FOR CUTTING UP DOG COLLAR)

TWIG FOR SPRINKLING HOLY WATER

KNIFE (TO SATISFY TRADE DESCRIPTIONS ACT)

MICRO-CHALICE

RADIO MICROPHONE

CHURCH MASTER KEY

USB DRIVE CONTAINING SERMON NOTES AND MP3s OF HYMNS

STICK WITH NOTCHES IN IT. (I DO NOT KNOW WHAT THESE SIGNIFY)

I CALLED PASTORALLY BUT YOU WERE NOT IN

UMBRELLAS

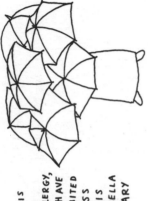

DURING WET
WEATHER
PEOPLE LEAVE
AN UMBRELLA
AT THE CHURCH
PORCH AS AN
ALTERNATIVE
TO PUTTING
SOMETHING INTO
THE COLLECTION

THIS IS
GREAT
FOR CLERGY,
WHO HAVE
UNLIMITED
ACCESS
TO THIS
UMBRELLA
LIBRARY

THEY CAN
USUALLY
FIND AN
UMBRELLA
TO MATCH
ANY ONE
OF THEIR
OUTFITS

CLERGY UMBRELLAS SINCE 1921

IT IS NOT
SUCH GOOD
NEWS FOR
THOSE
WHO HAVE
DEVOTED
THEIR LIVES
TO THE
CLERICAL
RAINWEAR
TRADE

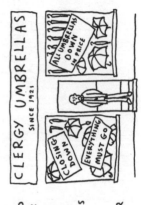

ALL UMBRELLAS DOWN IN PRICE

CLOSING DOWN

EVERYTHING MUST GO

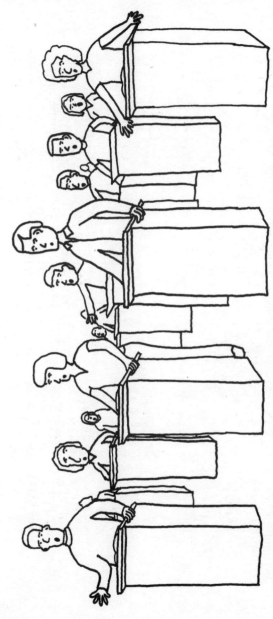

ANGLICAN ORDINANDS LEARN TO SPEAK FROM LECTERNS USING THE SPECIAL "REVERENT AND TERRIBLY APPROPRIATE" CLERGY VOICE

CLERICAL VESTMENTS

THE BEST WAY TO GAIN AN UNDERSTANDING OF THE VESTMENTS WORN BY CLERGY OF DIFFERENT CHURCHMANSHIPS WOULD (ONE IMAGINES) BE TO LOOK AT THEIR WASHING LINES:

LOW CHURCH: BOXER SHORTS, HOODIE, TIE, BASEBALL CAP, SUIT, CHUNKY SWEATER, ALL-PURPOSE ROBE (FOR THE BISHOP'S VISIT), FOOTBALL SCARF, T-SHIRT (JESUS)

HIGH CHURCH: UNDER-PANTS IN LITURGICALLY CORRECT COLOURS, ALB (HOODED), STOLE, ALB (NON-HOODED), BIRETTA, CASSOCK, CHASUBLE, SURPLICE, MANIPLE, T-SHIRT (WALSINGHAM)

THERE MAY BE SOME INACCURACIES IN SOME OF THE VESTMENT DRAWINGS. THIS DEMONSTRATES THAT I HAVE NOT SPENT VERY MUCH TIME LOOKING AT CLERGY WASHING LINES

DAYS OFF

WHAT THE CLERGY DO

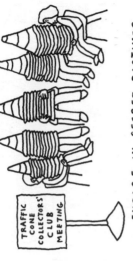

WRITE THINGS ABOUT THEIR
CONGREGATIONS ON THE INTERNET

KEEP AN EYE ON THE PARISHIONERS
TO MAKE SURE THEY ARE ADHERING
TO THE MESSAGE OF SUNDAY'S SERMON

ENGAGE IN SECRET PASTIMES

WATCH TV

THE INTERREGNUM

THIS IS THE TIME BETWEEN THE END OF ONE VICAR
AND THE START OF THE NEXT ONE

GOOD THINGS ABOUT AN INTERREGNUM

YOU DON'T HAVE TO WEAR ALL OF THE PROPER ROBES ETC

YOU CAN DO SOMETHING ELSE INSTEAD OF HAVING A SERMON

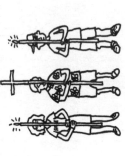

HEY... LET'S ALL GO AND RUN AROUND THE CHURCHYARD

BAD THINGS ABOUT AN INTERREGNUM

SERVICES ARE CONDUCTED BY VISITING CLERGY WITH PECULIAR METHODS

TODAY'S SERMON WILL BE CONDUCTED VIA THE MEDIUM OF DANCE... AND I'D LIKE EVERYONE TO JOIN IN...

MEMBERS OF THE CONGREGATION HAVE TO DO THINGS

CLERGY ADVERTISEMENTS

UNDERSTANDING THE HIDDEN SYMBOLISM

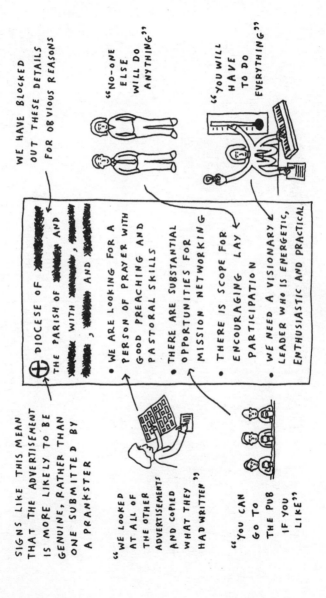

SIGNS LIKE THIS MEAN THAT THE ADVERTISEMENT IS MORE LIKELY TO BE GENUINE, RATHER THAN ONE SUBMITTED BY A PRANKSTER

"WE LOOKED AT ALL OF THE OTHER ADVERTISEMENTS AND COPIED WHAT THEY HAD WRITTEN"

"YOU CAN GO TO THE PUB IF YOU LIKE"

WE HAVE BLOCKED OUT THESE DETAILS FOR OBVIOUS REASONS

"NO-ONE ELSE WILL DO ANYTHING"

"YOU WILL HAVE TO DO EVERYTHING"

DIOCESE OF ▓▓▓▓ AND
THE PARISH OF ▓▓▓▓ WITH ▓▓▓▓,
▓▓▓▓, AND ▓▓▓▓

- WE ARE LOOKING FOR A PERSON OF PRAYER WITH GOOD PREACHING AND PASTORAL SKILLS
- THERE ARE SUBSTANTIAL OPPORTUNITIES FOR MISSION NETWORKING
- THERE IS SCOPE FOR ENCOURAGING LAY PARTICIPATION
- WE NEED A VISIONARY LEADER WHO IS ENERGETIC, ENTHUSIASTIC AND PRACTICAL

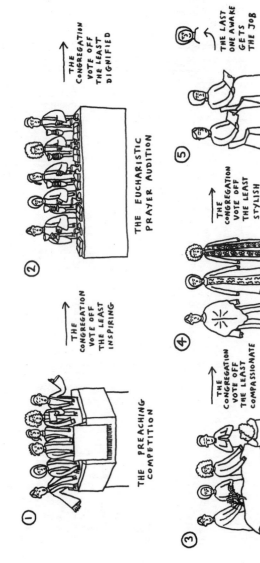

APPOINTING A NEW VICAR

THE PROCESS IS LONG AND COMPLEX

① THE PREACHING COMPETITION

THE CONGREGATION VOTE OFF THE LEAST INSPIRING →

② THE EUCHARISTIC PRAYER AUDITION

THE CONGREGATION VOTE OFF THE LEAST DIGNIFIED →

③ THE 'VISITING THE SICK' TEST

THE CONGREGATION VOTE OFF THE LEAST COMPASSIONATE →

④ THE ROBING CONTEST

THE CONGREGATION VOTE OFF THE LEAST STYLISH →

⑤ THE CHURCH MEETING CHALLENGE

THE LAST ONE AWAKE GETS THE JOB →

NON-STIPENDIARY MINISTERS

THESE ARE MINISTERS WHO DO NOT RECEIVE A STIPEND

BUT ARE PAID BY OTHER MEANS:

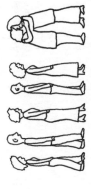

HUGS

QUITE OFTEN THE JOB
IS ITS OWN REWARD

INVITATIONS TO LUNCH
AT THE VICARAGE

THEIR NAME IN PRINT
IN THE NOTICE SHEET

HOUSE FOR DUTY

THE HOUSE RECEIVED DEPENDS UPON THE DUTIES UNDERTAKEN

EXTINGUISHING THE
CANDLES AT THE END
OF THE SERVICE

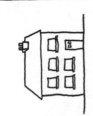

EXTINGUISHING THE
CANDLES AT THE END
OF THE SERVICE,
BAPTISMS, WEDDINGS,
FUNERALS, PREACHING,
LEADING SERVICES,
PASTORAL VISITING

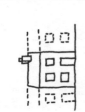

EXTINGUISHING THE
CANDLES AT THE END
OF THE SERVICE,
BAPTISMS, WEDDINGS,
FUNERALS, PREACHING,
LEADING SERVICES,
PASTORAL VISITING,
BEING IN CHARGE
OF THE SUNDAY
SCHOOL ROTA

EXTINGUISHING THE
CANDLES AT THE END
OF THE SERVICE,
BAPTISMS, WEDDINGS,
FUNERALS, PREACHING,
LEADING SERVICES,
PASTORAL VISITING,
BEING IN CHARGE
OF THE SUNDAY
SCHOOL ROTA,
FINDING A WAY TO
ENCOURAGE ALL OF
THE INVITED BISHOPS
TO ATTEND THE
LAMBETH CONFERENCE

THE LAITY

HOW TO RECOGNISE THEM

THE TWO TYPES OF PEOPLE:

CLERGY (ORDAINED PEOPLE)   LAITY (ORDINARY PEOPLE)

BUT HOW DO YOU TELL THEM APART?

THE MAKING OF NON-LITURGICAL HAND GESTURES
PROBABLY LAITY

SHALL WE GO OUT ON SATURDAY NIGHT?

I'M SORRY - I HAVE TO STAY IN AND WORK ON A FIFTEEN MINUTE SPEECH BASED LOOSELY ON THE BIBLE

MORE LIKELY TO BE CLERGY

WEARING A PATTERNED CASSOCK ALMOST CERTAINLY LAITY

TRICK QUESTION →

GOING ABOUT THEIR BUSINESS IN AN EVERYDAY FASHION WITHOUT ANY PARTICULAR DISTINGUISHING FEATURES

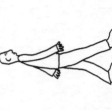

COULD BE LAITY OR PLAIN CLOTHES CLERGY

THE DIVISION OF LABOUR

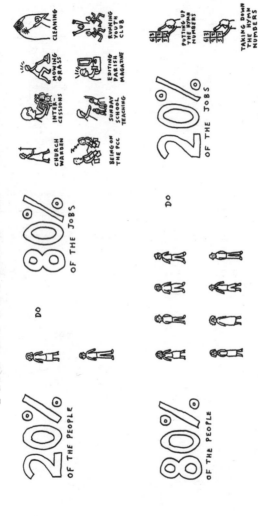

20% OF THE PEOPLE DO 80% OF THE JOBS

CHURCH WARDEN · INTER-CESSIONS · MOWING GRASS · CLEANING

BEING ON THE PCC · SUNDAY SCHOOL TEACHING · EDITING PARISH MAGAZINE · RUNNING YOUTH CLUB

80% OF THE PEOPLE DO 20% OF THE JOBS

PUTTING UP THE HYMN NUMBERS

TAKING DOWN THE HYMN NUMBERS

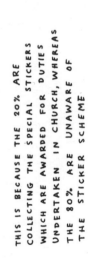

STICKER BOOK

THIS IS BECAUSE THE 20% ARE COLLECTING THE SPECIAL STICKERS WHICH ARE AWARDED FOR DUTIES UNDERTAKEN IN CHURCH, WHEREAS THE 80% ARE UNAWARE OF THE STICKER SCHEME

COMMISSIONING

ON THIS OCCASION THOSE WHO HAVE VOLUNTEERED TO TAKE ON A ROLE WITHIN THE LIFE OF THE CHURCH HAVE THE OPPORTUNITY TO SHAKE THE VICAR'S HAND. THEIR DUTIES ARE AS FOLLOWS:

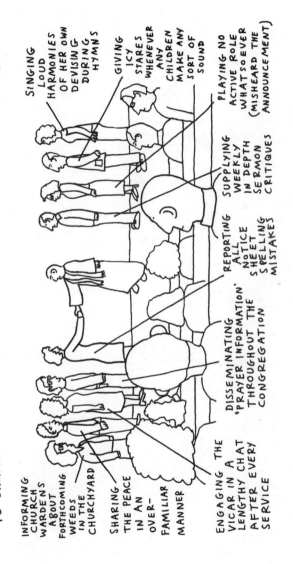

SINGING LOUD HARMONIES OF HER OWN DEVISING DURING HYMNS

GIVING ICY STARES WHENEVER ANY CHILDREN MAKE ANY SORT OF SOUND

PLAYING NO ACTIVE ROLE WHATSOEVER (MISHEARD THE ANNOUNCEMENT)

SUPPLYING WEEKLY IN DEPTH SERMON CRITIQUES

REPORTING ALL NOTICE SHEET SPELLING MISTAKES

DISSEMINATING 'PRAYER INFORMATION' THROUGHOUT THE CONGREGATION

INFORMING CHURCH WARDENS ABOUT FORTHCOMING WEEDS IN THE CHURCHYARD

SHARING THE PEACE IN AN OVER-FAMILIAR MANNER

ENGAGING THE VICAR IN A LENGTHY CHAT AFTER EVERY SERVICE

THE ELECTORAL ROLL

THIS IS A LIST OF ALL OF THE PEOPLE WHO ARE MEMBERS OF THE CHURCH ALONG WITH THOSE WHO ARE TRYING TO GET THEIR CHILDREN INTO THE CHURCH SCHOOL

ADVANTAGES OF A SMALL ELECTORAL ROLL

THERE IS LESS PARISH SHARE TO PAY

THERE IS NOT AS MUCH PASTORAL CARE TO BE UNDERTAKEN

QUEUE HERE FOR PASTORAL CARE 14 HOURS WAIT FROM THIS POINT

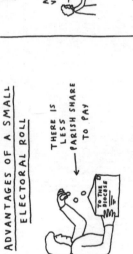

THERE IS A GREATER CHANCE THAT YOU WILL SEE SOMEONE THAT YOU RECOGNISE IN CHURCH

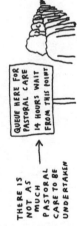

ADVANTAGES OF A LARGE ELECTORAL ROLL

THERE ARE LOTS OF PEOPLE TO DO THINGS

ANY VOLUNTEERS?

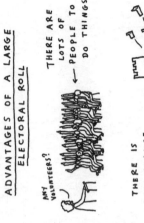

THERE IS LESS CHANCE OF BEING MERGED WITH A NEIGHBOURING PARISH

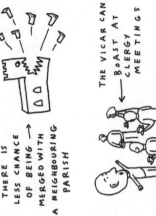

THE VICAR CAN BOAST AT CLERGY MEETINGS

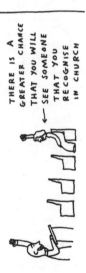

THE CHOIR

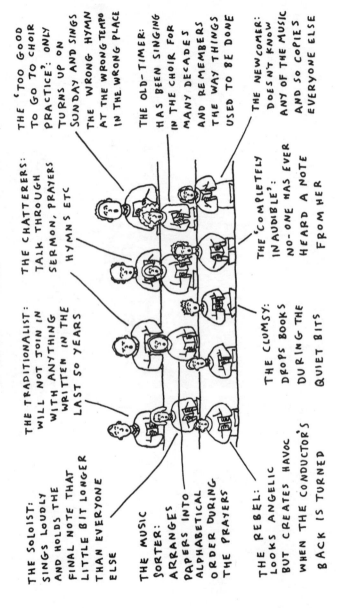

THE SOLOIST:
SINGS LOUDLY
AND HOLDS THE
FINAL NOTE THAT
LITTLE BIT LONGER
THAN EVERYONE
ELSE

THE MUSIC
SORTER:
ARRANGES
PAPERS INTO
ALPHABETICAL
ORDER DURING
THE PRAYERS

THE REBEL:
LOOKS ANGELIC
BUT CREATES HAVOC
WHEN THE CONDUCTOR'S
BACK IS TURNED

THE TRADITIONALIST:
WILL NOT JOIN IN
WITH ANYTHING
WRITTEN IN THE
LAST 50 YEARS

THE CLUMSY:
DROPS BOOKS
DURING THE
QUIET BITS

THE CHATTERERS:
TALK THROUGH
SERMON, PRAYERS
HYMNS ETC

THE 'COMPLETELY
INAUDIBLE':
NO-ONE HAS EVER
HEARD A NOTE
FROM HER

THE 'TOO GOOD
TO GO TO CHOIR
PRACTICE': ONLY
TURNS UP ON
SUNDAY AND SINGS
THE WRONG HYMN
AT THE WRONG TEMPO
IN THE WRONG PLACE

THE OLD-TIMER:
HAS BEEN SINGING
IN THE CHOIR FOR
MANY DECADES
AND REMEMBERS
THE WAY THINGS
USED TO BE DONE

THE NEWCOMER:
DOESN'T KNOW
ANY OF THE MUSIC
AND SO COPIES
EVERYONE ELSE

SUNDAY SCHOOL

WHAT THE PARENTS THINK
HAPPENS AT SUNDAY SCHOOL

WHAT ACTUALLY HAPPENS
AT SUNDAY SCHOOL

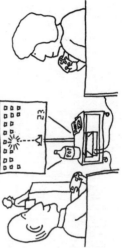

WHAT THE CHILDREN THINK
HAPPENS IN THE MAIN CHURCH SERVICE

WHAT ACTUALLY HAPPENS
IN THE MAIN CHURCH SERVICE

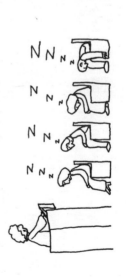

THE CRÈCHE

A SIMPLIFIED ORDER OF SERVICE IS FOLLOWED

PROCESSING IN

THE SERMON

SHARING THE PEACE

PROCESSING OUT

THE FLOWER LADIES

FEATURES OF THEIR SECRET COMMON ROOM

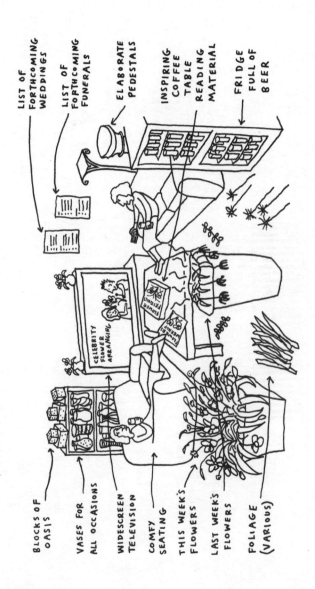

LIST OF FORTHCOMING WEDDINGS

LIST OF FORTHCOMING FUNERALS

ELABORATE PEDESTALS

INSPIRING COFFEE TABLE READING MATERIAL

FRIDGE FULL OF BEER

BLOCKS OF OASIS

VASES FOR ALL OCCASIONS

WIDESCREEN TELEVISION

COMFY SEATING

THIS WEEK'S FLOWERS

LAST WEEK'S FLOWERS

FOLIAGE (VARIOUS)

CELEBRITY FLOWER ARRANGING

THE HOME GROUP

THE HOME GROUP (OR HOUSE GROUP, OR CELL GROUP, OR SMALL GROUP) MEETS ON A MID-WEEK EVENING TO UNDERTAKE BIBLE STUDY AND DISCUSSION. THESE ARE THE PEOPLE YOU WILL FIND THERE

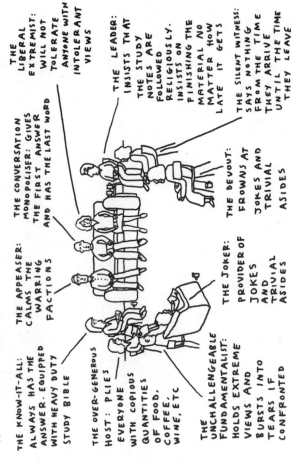

THE KNOW-IT-ALL:
ALWAYS HAS THE
ANSWER. EQUIPPED
WITH HEAVY DUTY
STUDY BIBLE

THE OVER-GENEROUS
HOST: PLIES
EVERYONE
WITH COPIOUS
QUANTITIES
OF FOOD,
COFFEE,
WINE, ETC

THE
UNCHALLENGEABLE
FUNDAMENTALIST:
HOLDS EXTREME
VIEWS AND
BURSTS INTO
TEARS IF
CONFRONTED

THE APPEASER:
CALMS THE
WARRING
FACTIONS

THE JOKER:
PROVIDER OF
JOKES
AND
TRIVIAL
ASIDES

THE CONVERSATION
MONOPOLISER: GIVES
THE FIRST ANSWER
AND HAS THE LAST WORD

THE DEVOUT:
FROWNS AT
JOKES AND
TRIVIAL
ASIDES

THE
LIBERAL
EXTREMIST:
WILL NOT
TOLERATE
ANYONE WITH
INTOLERANT
VIEWS

THE LEADER:
INSISTS THAT
THE STUDY
NOTES ARE
FOLLOWED
RELIGIOUSLY.
INSISTS ON
FINISHING THE
MATERIAL NO
MATTER HOW
LATE IT GETS

THE SILENT WITNESS:
SAYS NOTHING
FROM THE TIME
THEY ARRIVE
UNTIL THE TIME
THEY LEAVE

CARING FOR THE ENVIRONMENT

CHURCHES ARE DOING ALL SORTS OF THINGS TO BE ENVIRONMENTALLY FRIENDLY

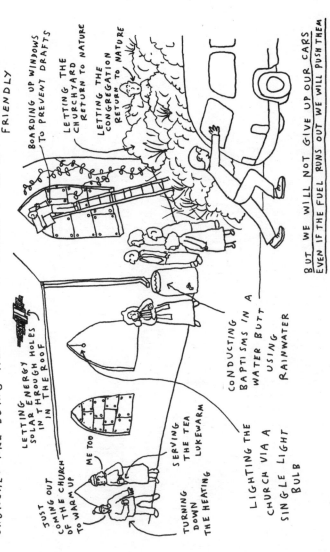

BOARDING UP WINDOWS TO PREVENT DRAFTS

LETTING THE CHURCHYARD RETURN TO NATURE

LETTING THE CONGREGATION RETURN TO NATURE

LETTING ENERGY SOLAR THROUGH HOLES IN THE ROOF

JUST COMING OUT OF THE CHURCH TO WARM UP

ME TOO

SERVING THE TEA LUKEWARM

TURNING DOWN THE HEATING

LIGHTING THE CHURCH VIA A SINGLE LIGHT BULB

CONDUCTING BAPTISMS IN A WATER BUTT USING RAINWATER

BUT WE WILL NOT GIVE UP OUR CARS EVEN IF THE FUEL RUNS OUT WE WILL PUSH THEM

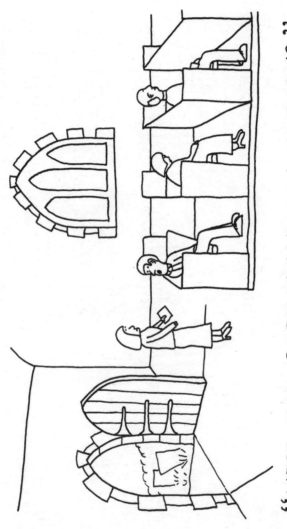

"WERE YOU BORN AGAIN IN A BARN?"

OUTREACH

THIS IS WHERE WE GATHER TOGETHER AT THE CHURCH AND HOPE THAT
SOMEONE COMES IN. THESE ARE SOME COMMON OUTREACH METHODS:

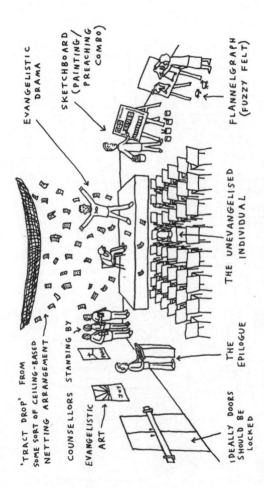

'TRACT DROP' FROM
SOME SORT OF CEILING-BASED
NETTING ARRANGEMENT

COUNSELLORS STANDING BY

EVANGELISTIC
ART

EVANGELISTIC
DRAMA

SKETCHBOARD
(PAINTING/
PREACHING
COMBO)

FLANNELGRAPH
(FUZZY FELT)

THE UNEVANGELISED
INDIVIDUAL

THE
EPILOGUE

IDEALLY DOORS
SHOULD BE
LOCKED

THESE PROCEDURES MAY BE COMBINED WITH COFFEE (COFFEE MORNING)
SINGING (SEEKER SERVICE) OR FOOD (ALPHA COURSE) IF YOU LIKE

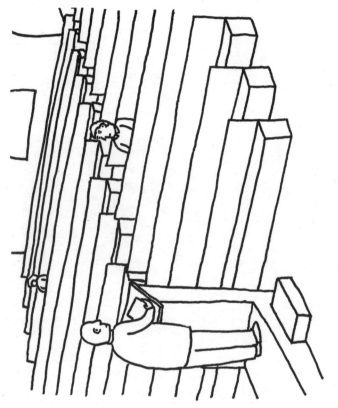

IT IS NOT ABOUT THE NUMBERS

THE FIVE MARKS OF MISSION

1. BRUISE RECEIVED WHILST MINGLING MISSIONALLY AT 'THE CROWN' WITH SOME EVANGELISTIC PAMPHLETS

2. BITE FROM DOG AS A RESULT OF DOOR-TO-DOOR NURTURING WORK

3. CRUSHED TOE CAUSED BY A BAKED BEAN TIN FALLING FROM A GREAT HEIGHT AT THE SOUP KITCHEN

4. HEAD INJURY SUSTAINED WHILST ATTEMPTING TO TRANSFORM THE UNJUST STRUCTURES OF THE QUEUING SYSTEM AT THE FOOTBALL GROUND

5. SCRATCHES CAUSED BY MY ATTEMPT TO STRIVE TO SAFEGUARD THE INTEGRITY OF AN OVERGROWN FLOWERBED AND SUSTAIN AND RENEW THE LIFE OF THE PATIO AREA

THE ORGAN RECITAL

72 of 96

THE ORGAN RECITAL

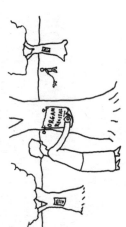

WE HAVE GOOD NEWS TO SHARE:
THERE IS AN ORGAN RECITAL
ON WEDNESDAY AT LUNCHTIME

WE WILL MAKE THE MESSAGE
KNOWN IN THE LIBRARY

WE WILL GO FORTH AND PUT SOME
A4 PHOTOCOPIED POSTERS IN THE PARK

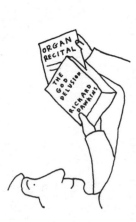

WE WILL NOT BE ASHAMED TO SPREAD
THE WORD VIA OUR APARTMENT WINDOWS

THE ALL-AGE SERVICE

THIS IS A SERVICE DESIGNED ESPECIALLY FOR CHILDREN. ESSENTIAL ELEMENTS INCLUDE:

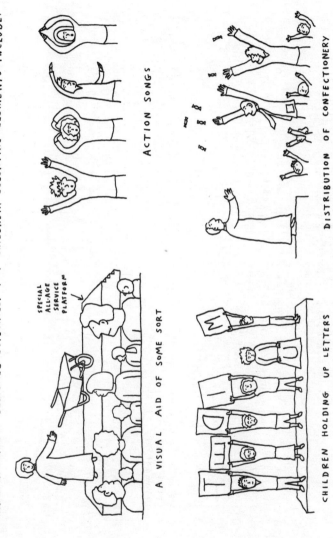

ACTION SONGS

DISTRIBUTION OF CONFECTIONERY

SPECIAL ALL-AGE SERVICE PLATFORM

A VISUAL AID OF SOME SORT

CHILDREN HOLDING UP LETTERS

THE SUNDAY SCHOOL SONG

THE CAMCORDER BRIGADE

HELPERS PROMPT ENTHUSIASTICALLY

THE LARGEST CHILDREN AND THOSE WHO DID NOT ATTEND THE PRACTICE ARE PLACED IN THE FRONT ROW

SUNDAY SCHOOL LEADERS SING WITH GREAT GUSTO

THE ANTI-CAMCORDER BRIGADE

OTHERS ARE DEEP IN REFLECTION (OR SLEEP)

CONGREGATION MEMBERS GRIN ENCOURAGINGLY

SMALLER CHILDREN AND THOSE SUSCEPTIBLE TO DISTRACTION ARE PLACED AT THE BACK

A MINOR SCUFFLE

EXCUSES FOR ABSENTEEISM

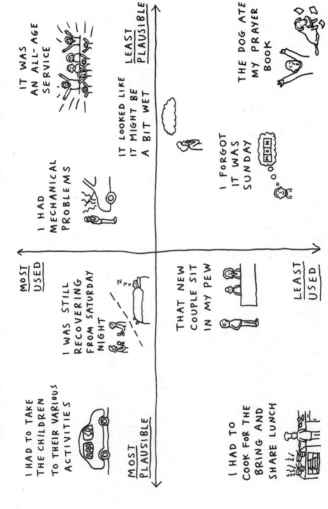

CHURCH V FOOTBALL

DECIDING WHETHER TO GO TO CHURCH OR THE FOOTBALL MATCH

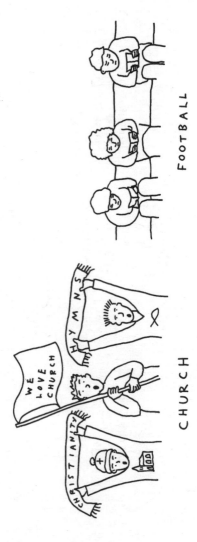

CHURCH   FOOTBALL

YOU NEED TO MAKE YOUR OWN MIND UP REALLY.

THERE IS NOTHING THAT I COULD SAY THAT IS GOING

TO CONVINCE YOU ONE WAY OR THE OTHER

71

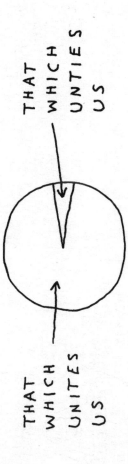

DEANERY SYNOD

DEANERY SYNOD IS HELD IN AN OBSCURE
CHURCH HALL MILES FROM ANYWHERE

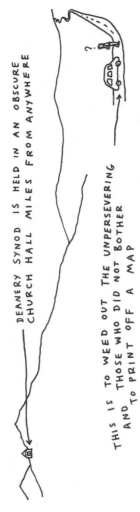

THIS IS TO WEED OUT THE UNPERSEVERING
AND THOSE WHO DID NOT BOTHER
TO PRINT OFF A MAP

IF AN AGREEMENT CANNOT
BE REACHED A WRESTLING MATCH
TAKES PLACE BETWEEN
THE CHURCH TREASURERS

DEBATES ARE CONDUCTED
OVER THE LEVELS OF
PARISH SHARE TO BE PAID
BY THE DIFFERENT CHURCHES

RURAL DEANS

RURAL DEANS ARE IN CHARGE OF RURAL DEANERIES. THEIR DUTIES ARE AS FOLLOWS:

CALLING THE CLERGY TOGETHER
FOR DEANERY CHAPTER MEETINGS

SUPERVISING THE PROVISION OF SUNDAY
SERVICES DURING AN INTERREGNUM

CARING FOR THE CLERGY
OF THE DEANERY

PROVIDING A MEANS OF COMMUNICATION
BETWEEN THE PARISHES AND THE BISHOP

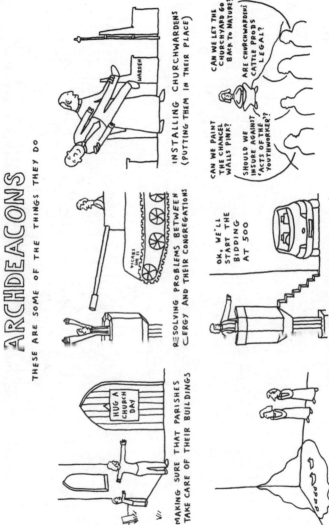

BISHOPS
WHAT THEY DO

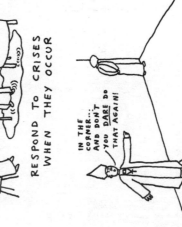

KEEP THAT HOLE PLUGGED BISHOP - I'M SURE THE PLUMBER WILL BE HERE SOON

RESPOND TO CRISES WHEN THEY OCCUR

THE DIOCESAN CALCULATOR

THE DIOCESAN CORKSCREW

THE DIOCESAN ADJUSTABLE SPANNER

THE DIOCESAN YOUTH OFFICER

CURRENTLY IN USE

TAKE RESPONSIBILITY FOR THE DIOCESAN PORTFOLIO OF ASSETS

IN THE CORNER... AND DON'T YOU DARE DO THAT AGAIN!

DISCIPLINE THE CLERGY

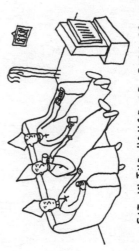

SIT IN THE HOUSE OF BISHOPS

WHAT REALLY HAPPENS AT BISHOPS' MEETINGS

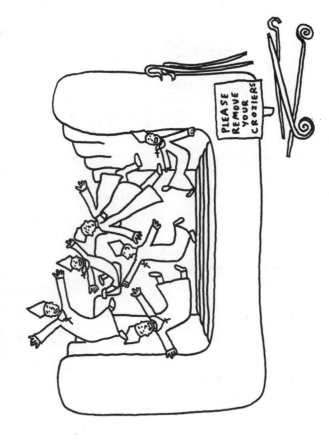

CATHEDRALS

SHOULD WE CHARGE VISITORS? THERE ARE A NUMBER OF DIFFERENT APPROACHES:

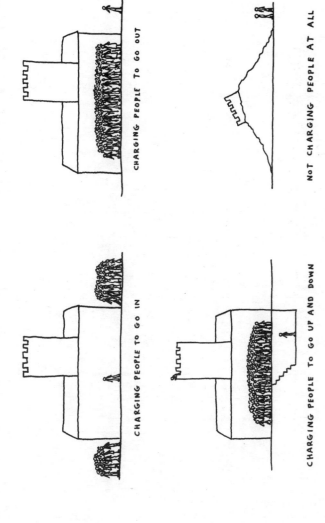

CHARGING PEOPLE TO GO IN

CHARGING PEOPLE TO GO OUT

CHARGING PEOPLE TO GO UP AND DOWN

NOT CHARGING PEOPLE AT ALL

THE RELIGIOUS BOOKSHOP

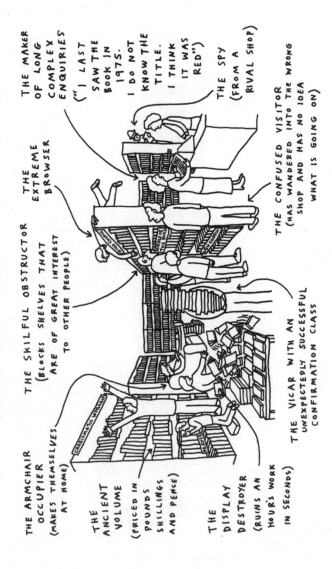

THE ARMCHAIR OCCUPIER
(MAKES THEMSELVES AT HOME)

THE ANCIENT VOLUME
(PRICED IN POUNDS SHILLINGS AND PENCE)

THE DISPLAY DESTROYER
(RUINS AN HOUR'S WORK IN SECONDS)

THE SKILFUL OBSTRUCTOR
(BLOCKS SHELVES THAT ARE OF GREAT INTEREST TO OTHER PEOPLE)

THE EXTREME BROWSER

THE MAKER OF LONG COMPLEX ENQUIRIES
("I LAST SAW THE BOOK IN 1975. I DO NOT KNOW THE TITLE. I THINK IT WAS RED")

THE SPY (FROM A RIVAL SHOP)

THE CONFUSED VISITOR (HAS WANDERED INTO THE WRONG SHOP AND HAS NO IDEA WHAT IS GOING ON)

THE VICAR WITH AN UNEXPECTEDLY SUCCESSFUL CONFIRMATION CLASS

GENERAL SYNOD

AS OBSERVED FROM A LOFTY VANTAGEPOINT

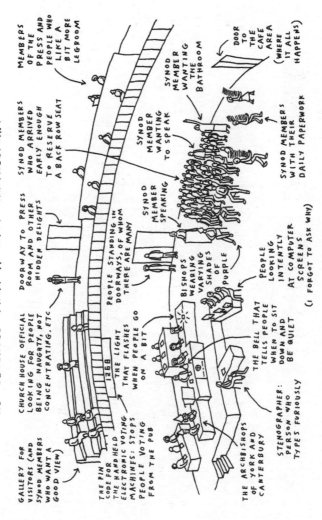

GALLERY FOR VISITORS (AND SYNOD MEMBERS WHO WANT A GOOD VIEW)

CHURCH HOUSE OFFICIAL LOOKING FOR PEOPLE BEING NAUGHTY, NOT CONCENTRATING, ETC

DOORWAY TO PRESS ROOM AND OTHER HIDDEN DELIGHTS

SYNOD MEMBERS WHO ARRIVED EARLY ENOUGH TO RESERVE A BACK ROW SEAT

MEMBERS OF THE PRESS AND PEOPLE WHO LIKE A BIT MORE LEGROOM

THE PIN CODE FOR THE HANDHELD ELECTRONIC VOTING MACHINES: STOPS PEOPLE VOTING FROM THE PUB

THE LIGHT THAT FLASHES WHEN PEOPLE GO ON A BIT

PEOPLE STANDING IN DOORWAYS, OF WHOM THERE ARE MANY

SYNOD MEMBER SPEAKING

SYNOD MEMBER WANTING TO SPEAK

SYNOD MEMBER WANTING THE BATHROOM

DOOR TO THE CAFE AREA (WHERE IT ALL HAPPENS)

SYNOD MEMBERS WITH THEIR DAILY PAPERWORK

BISHOPS WEARING VARYING SHADES OF PURPLE

PEOPLE LOOKING INTENTLY AT COMPUTER SCREENS (I FORGOT TO ASK WHY)

THE BELL THAT TELLS PEOPLE WHEN TO SIT DOWN AND BE QUIET

STENOGRAPHER: PERSON WHO TYPES FURIOUSLY

THE ARCHBISHOPS OF YORK AND CANTERBURY

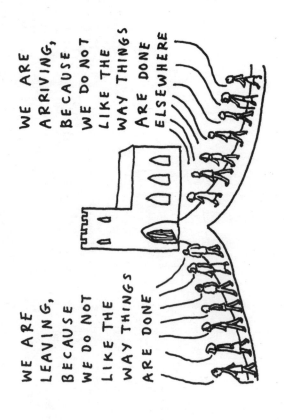

80

NEW YEAR'S RESOLUTIONS

THESE CAN BE CUT OUT AND KEPT IN THE PAGES OF YOUR LECTIONARY

FINISH SERMONS BEFORE THE EARLY HOURS OF SUNDAY MORNING	SAY MORNING PRAYER WITH GREATER ENTHUSIASM	WALK TO CHURCH MORE OFTEN
ARRIVE AT CHURCH ON TIME	SAY MORNING PRAYER	WALK OUT OF CHURCH MORE OFTEN
GET ON TO THE PCC	SPEND MORE TIME WITH THE FAMILY	LOSE WEIGHT
GET OFF THE PCC	SPEND LESS TIME WITH THE FAMILY	LOSE DEAD WEIGHT (FROM CHURCH, PCC, ETC)
GET INTO FEWER DEBATES ABOUT THE STATE OF GLOBAL ANGLICANISM	VOLUNTEER A BIT MORE	TIDY THE SECOND BEDROOM
GET INTO MORE DEBATES ABOUT THE STATE OF GLOBAL ANGLICANISM	VOLUNTEER A BIT LESS	STOP THROWING SNAILS INTO NEXT DOOR'S GARDEN

ASH WEDNESDAY

THE PALM CROSSES
LEFT OVER FROM
LAST YEAR'S PALM
SUNDAY SERVICE
(OWING TO SLIGHTLY
OPTIMISTIC ORDERING)
ARE THE PRINCIPAL
INGREDIENT

PALM
CROSSES

SOME CONGREGATION MEMBERS
WEAR THE SIGN OF THE CROSS
ON THEIR FOREHEADS THROUGHOUT
THE WEEK TO PROVE THAT
THEY ATTENDED THE SERVICE

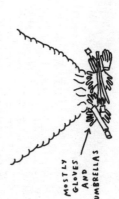

AND TO SHOW THAT THEY DO NOT
WASH THAT REGULARLY

SOME ASH IS MADE USING
A SECRET RECIPE THAT HAS
BEEN HANDED DOWN BY MANY
GENERATIONS OF CLERGY

SECRET
RECIPES
HANDED
DOWN BY
MANY
GENERATIONS
OF CLERGY

IF THERE ARE NOT MANY
PALM CROSSES LEFT OVER THEN
OTHER ITEMS THAT HAVE BEEN
LEFT IN CHURCH CAN BE BURNT

MOSTLY
GLOVES
AND
UMBRELLAS

84

MOTHERING SUNDAY

THERE HAS BEEN CONCERN IN CERTAIN CIRCLES THAT PEOPLE HAVE BEEN
STARTING TO CALL THIS ANCIENT FESTIVAL 'MOTHER'S DAY' INSTEAD OF
'MOTHERING SUNDAY'. I THEREFORE PROPOSE THE FOLLOWING ACTIONS:

THE SETTING UP
OF A WEBSITE

THE SIGNING OF
A PETITION

THE LOBBYING
OF PARLIAMENT

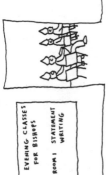

THE WRITING OF STATEMENTS
BY SOME BISHOPS

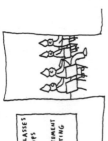

OCCASIONAL ATTENDERS

EXAMPLES OF 'TWICE A YEAR' CHURCHGOERS

WE ONLY GO AT CHRISTMAS AND EASTER — FOR THE KIDS MAINLY

WE TEND TO GO ON THE THIRD SUNDAY OF EPIPHANY AND THE SIXTEENTH SUNDAY AFTER TRINITY — I DON'T KNOW WHY REALLY — IT'S JUST A HABIT WE'VE GOT INTO

WE GO WHEN IT IS A PARADE SERVICE — MOTHER'S DAY AND REMEMBRANCE USUALLY

HOW TO ENCOURAGE THEM TO COME TO CHURCH A BIT MORE OFTEN

TELL THEM ABOUT THE GREAT TIMES WE HAVE DURING SERVICES FOR THE OTHER 50 WEEKS OF THE YEAR

WE REPLACE THE PEWS WITH RECLINING ARMCHAIRS

GLASSES OF WINE ARE SERVED

AND THE MONEY IS GIVEN OUT RATHER THAN BEING COLLECTED IN

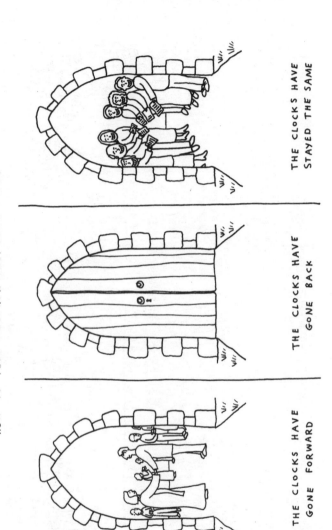

THE CLOCKS

HOW TO TELL WHETHER THEY HAVE CHANGED

THE CLOCKS HAVE
GONE FORWARD

THE CLOCKS HAVE
GONE BACK

THE CLOCKS HAVE
STAYED THE SAME

CHRISTINGLES

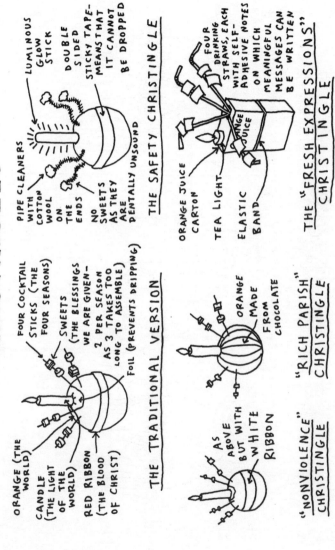

ORANGE (THE WORLD)

CANDLE (THE LIGHT OF THE WORLD)

RED RIBBON (THE BLOOD OF CHRIST)

FOUR COCKTAIL STICKS (THE FOUR SEASONS)

SWEETS (THE BLESSINGS WE ARE GIVEN — 2 PER SEASON AS 3 TAKES TOO LONG TO ASSEMBLE)

FOIL (PREVENTS DRIPPING)

THE TRADITIONAL VERSION

PIPE CLEANERS WITH COTTON WOOL ON THE ENDS

LUMINOUS GLOW STICK

DOUBLE SIDED STICKY TAPE- MEANS THAT IT CANNOT BE DROPPED

NO SWEETS AS THEY ARE DENTALLY UNSOUND

THE SAFETY CHRISTINGLE

ORANGE MADE FROM CHOCOLATE

"RICH PARISH" CHRISTINGLE

AS ABOVE BUT WITH WHITE RIBBON

"NONVIOLENCE" CHRISTINGLE

ORANGE JUICE CARTON

TEA LIGHT

ELASTIC BAND

FOUR DRINKING STRAWS, EACH WITH SELF- ADHESIVE NOTES ON WHICH MEANINGFUL MESSAGES CAN BE WRITTEN

ORANGE JUICE

THE "FRESH EXPRESSIONS" CHRISTINGLE

CAROL SERVICES

IT IS TRADITIONAL FOR THOSE WHO ATTEND CLERGY GATHERINGS TO DISPLAY
THE NUMBER OF CAROL SERVICES THEY EXPECT TO TAKE THIS YEAR

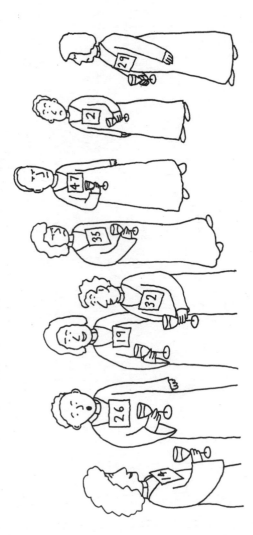

THOSE WITH SINGLE DIGIT FIGURES ARE FROWNED UPON MERCILESSLY

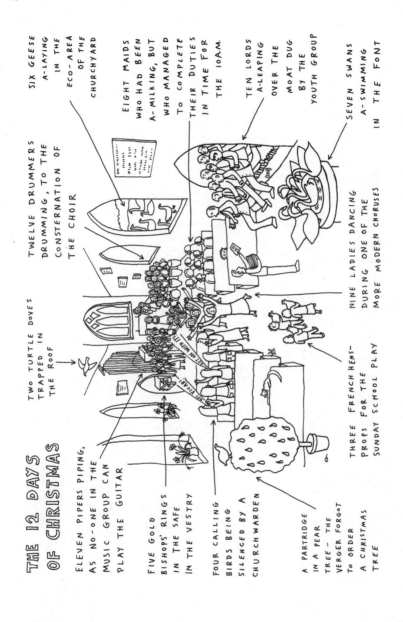

THE 12 DAYS OF CHRISTMAS

TWELVE DRUMMERS DRUMMING, TO THE CONSTERNATION OF THE CHOIR

SIX GEESE A-LAYING IN THE ECO-AREA OF THE CHURCHYARD

EIGHT MAIDS WHO HAD BEEN A-MILKING, BUT WHO MANAGED TO COMPLETE THEIR DUTIES IN TIME FOR THE 10A.M.

TEN LORDS A-LEAPING OVER THE MOAT DUG BY THE YOUTH GROUP

SEVEN SWANS A-SWIMMING IN THE FONT

TWO TURTLE DOVES TRAPPED IN THE ROOF

ELEVEN PIPERS PIPING, AS NO-ONE IN THE MUSIC GROUP CAN PLAY THE GUITAR

FIVE GOLD BISHOPS' RINGS IN THE SAFE IN THE VESTRY

FOUR CALLING BIRDS BEING SILENCED BY A CHURCHWARDEN

NINE LADIES DANCING DURING ONE OF THE MORE MODERN CHORUSES

A PARTRIDGE IN A PEAR TREE – THE VERGER FORGOT TO ORDER A CHRISTMAS TREE

THREE FRENCH HENS – PROPS FOR THE SUNDAY SCHOOL PLAY

LEAVING CHURCH

SOMETIMES IT CAN BE DIFFICULT TO ENCOURAGE PEOPLE TO LEAVE AFTER
A SERVICE BECAUSE THEY HAVE BEEN HAVING SUCH A GREAT TIME.
THESE ARE SOME OF THE TACTICS THAT THE CHURCHWARDENS ADOPT:

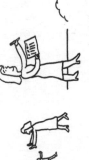

APPROACHING PEOPLE
WITH A ROTA

TURNING OUT THE LIGHTS

JANGLING KEYS

ORGANISING A
WORK PARTY

THE COMMENCEMENT
OF A GROUP HUG

SING WITH ME... SHINE ♪ JESUS ♪ SHINE ♪...

SOME ODD OR
UNPREDICTABLE BEHAVIOUR